December
in Cinnamon Bay

Balboa Press books may be ordered through booksellers or by contacting:

Balboa Press
A Division of Hay House
1663 Liberty Drive
Bloomington, IN 47403
www.balboapress.com
1 (877) 407-4847

ISBN: 978-1-9822-4155-1 (sc)
ISBN: 978-1-9822-4156-8 (e)

Library of Congress Control Number: 2020901217

Print information available on the last page.

Balboa Press rev. date: 02/06/2020

December
in Cinnamon Bay

by Sher Stone-Wightman

Dedications to my dear friends

Steven Finder is the photographer who supplied these lovely photos.

Laura Hernandez did the graphic design and placement for the cover.

I rise early one morning, not yet daybreak, to prepare for my new adventure, to visit a place I have heard so much about, but not yet seen.

Cinnamon Bay in St. John, the capital of the Island of Antigua, part of the Virgin Islands in the Caribbean.

I hop out of bed where I stay in St. Thomas. Going through my morning ritual of getting ready for my incredible adventure, I pack a few things: a towel, swimsuit, sunscreen and my favorite straw hat. Sunglasses and water, of course. Sandals or tennies? Oh, both-just in case. I'll wear the tennies and the rest goes in my tote.

Looking out the window I notice the sun making its appearance known along the waters edge. What an incredible view. The bright orange sun peeping out to greet the day against the contrast of the dark blue ocean waters. As the seconds pass, the sun gets larger and brighter. This is so much my favorite time of day. I don't want to miss any of it.

I gather my things and pickup my notebook and pencil that I almost forgot, toss them into my tote and head out the door to begin my walk to and along the sea wall.

Seagulls are wailing their song, greeting the day as well. So calm is the water and it looks like glass with the sun's reflection rising above it. So still and peaceful. Quiet is the city as just a few people are out and about.

It does not take long, as I walk a few blocks, for the city to be awakened by the early morning sun. By now, a complete circle of blaze.

Pedestrians, cars and scooters coming from many directions. Here transportation travels on the left side of the road. I hear sounds of turning wheels and motors running as vehicles are passing by. Sounds of scooters coming from all directions in their high pitch humming sound. Hurry-scurry to get somewhere. I wonder where they are all going?

How fun is this?

I continue to walk until I arrive. Arrive at the spot. The spot where the ferry meets the dock. The ferry to take me from St. Thomas to St. John.

Across the street is a great coffee shop. I walk across the now busy street to get some breakfast and coffee to go.

I enter the coffee shop and approach the counter while glancing over the many selections. I choose a wonderful slice of breakfast quiche and a cup of coffee with a shot of mocha and plenty of cream. It smells delightful, perfect for my ferry trip excursion.

Back across the street I go to the ferry spot. By now, others are waiting and a line is starting to form. I join in and start sipping on my very warm cup of coffee. Oh yes, just the right amount of mocha.

Excitement is stirring as more people arrive. Are they going to Cinnamon Bay as well? Looks like people from all walks of life. Sounds like people from many different lands, as I listen to various accents and languages being spoken.

The ferry is making its way towards the dock. A couple of men, one at each end, quickly secure the ferry to the dock.

One of the men, with tickets in hand, approaches the people in line. He announces. "Ferry to St. John!"

Quickly, one person at a time, we hand the ticket man money to board the ferry. Now it is my turn and I hand him the money and board as well. It's a double decker, which I prefer, hoping to get a seat on top.

I listen to the slow shuffling of our footsteps against the gangway as we all begin to board. On the ferry and up the stairs some of us go.

I find a great spot on the top deck to observe the incredible scenery. I take a seat and get situated and begin to take it all in, breathing deep to inhale the morning sea air.

This is definitely one of life's amazing pleasures.

Putting on my sunglasses and hat while feeling the warm morning sun kiss my skin, I then get out my breakfast of spinach and egg quiche and sip on my still warm coffee. Just perfect.

The captain turns the key to start the rumbling of the grinding Diesel engine. It takes a few minutes to warm up enough to pull away from the dock.

The horn blows to alert the passengers as we begin to move.

I watch the land sliding by ever so slowly as the ferry moves on.

Before long, the view of the land gets smaller and smaller. Other boats passing by and seagulls wailing overhead as they make their journey as well.

The weather is lovely, warm but not too hot. The ferry moving across the ocean waters, stirs a gentle breeze.

Time passes quickly in what seems a matter of minutes. I see the view of the island up ahead: The island of Antigua.

We approach a very large dock with ticket counters and many people waiting in line. Are they waiting to board this ferry? A couple of men secure the ferry to the dock and I begin gathering my things to get ready to deboard. All this happens very quickly.

All passengers stand, then begin walking in a shuffling manner, one after another until our feet touch the dock. Now continuing on until we all reach land.

My feet touch land and suddenly my senses are stimulated. Oh, my! There is more beyond the sight I see here. I feel an interesting and familiar energy. Not sure why or what; but it is old. Is it Cinnamon Bay? My destination?

Yes, it is definitely old. And I feel people. Lots and lots of people. Not knowing the history of St. John, I wonder. Maybe the native people from long, long ago.

Smells like some local tropical flowers nearby.

I look around viewing the buildings and shops on my right and some taxis and vans on my left. Dirt roads to travel by. Signs are pointing this way and that. A sign for Cinnamon Bay points to the left; so I walk that way.

A man approaches me and asks if I want a ride.

"Yes I do, to Cinnamon Bay!"

He walks me to his van and invites me to board. "We wait for others," he says.

Before long, more people arrive.

In time, enough passengers board the van for the transport. He collects the monies and off we go.

While making several stops along the way, I look out the window to notice the scenery. Very lush and thick is the vegetation here, dark green local palm trees and other tropical plants. Beautiful flowering bushes. Some look like Bougainvilleas in various intense vivid colors. Vines dangling here and there.

"Cinnamon Bay," he announces as he looks at me through his rear view mirror. I re-gather my things and step off the van.

More signs ahead. Sugar Factory to the right and beach to the left. What is this Sugar Factory all about? I take a few minutes to read the history: Cinnamon Bay Estate. Early 1700s. Most prosperous sugar cane factory on the island. There is an old rock building in the distance through the lush vegetation. That must be the remains of the sugar cane factory. This is something I must check out.

I walk on the grounds surrounding what is left of this old structure, trying to imagine how sugar was made from the cane long ago. My olfactory glands ignite with the smells of the remains of the sugar on the cane. Watching my steps carefully as it appears not many people have been through here. Quite a rugged terrain.

Oh, and there it goes again. That energy. That energy I felt when I arrived. Yes, it is definitely stronger here. Yes! Yes! This is it, the energy is the people in the factory.

Oh my! I look down at my watch and notice the time. It is mid-morning, I do want to get to the beach. Another day, another time. I will come back to this place.

I now take the path to the left. The path to the beach. Tall slender palms surround me as I walk down the sandy dirt trail. Never have I seen anything like this before. Long stringy vines coming down these palm trees, for climbing perhaps? I feel my inner little-girlness want to come out to play. Wondering about swinging and climbing up a vine. How fun that would be.

I notice a skip in my walk as I proceed along the trail.

Crossing a street I notice a man on a scooter wearing a helmet, smiling at me as he goes by. I wonder where he is going?

As I get closer, I hear music coming from a nearby taxi playing "Candle in the Wind," with a Caribbean flair. Amazing. One of my favorite songs. But it is not by the original artist.

A local man sitting on a bench says "Hello Cinderella."

I respond with "Hello." He asks my name and I ask his.

"Spencer," he says. "Have a wonderful day."

"Oh yes. I am. You too, Spencer."

He comments on my wonderful straw hat. "Thank you."

I continue along another trail that says to the beach. Sand and incredible blue waters are peeping through the vegetation. More beautiful flowering bushes and their scent is quite intoxicating. There is a stone building to my right which is a bathhouse for changing and such. I enter and change into my beach wear. A child's voice in the neighboring stall is sharing her excitement. She is expressing my feelings exactly today.

I proceed to the beach and approach the sand. I remove my sandals to feel the sand beneath my feet and in between my toes. This sand is very fine in texture and soft light griege in color.

Walking slowly while looking for the perfect spot. I notice a quiet more secluded area. It seems just perfect. When I stop, my feet sink into the sand. Very nice.

It is a nice flat area which is perfect for sunbathing, people watching and ocean viewing. I place my towel onto the sand facing the direction of the ocean view. As I am getting settled I notice several sailboats. Looks like Hobiecats. Appears they are for rent. Two men are looking at one of the boats. I cannot hear them but can clearly see what they are doing. Another young man in his mid to late twenties, comes up to talk to them. He looks American and is very fit and tan, wearing only swim trunks. He has shoulder length curly hair of ringlets in blonde and light brown gently caressing his bronzed and glistening skin. He is in charge of the Hobiecat rentals. The three talk a bit then the two men take off. I wonder if they are gathering what they will need for their trip.

While observing the men I apply my sunscreen so I can lie out a bit. I do love how the sun touches my skin in a warm gentle way. As the day moves on it will be warmer and then I will have that sweat and saltiness that I enjoy as well. This is a great opportunity to get a winter tan, since it is much colder where I come from.

As I wait on the sailors, I look off into the ocean. The water is dark blue and full of waves. I see many different islands and various sailboats in the distance. The islands are covered with very dark green foliage. The sailboats don beautifully colored sails. All contrasting against the light-colored sun and beautiful blue skies with just a few fluffy clouds.

It is not crowded here, maybe because of the time of year. Some people are lying out like myself taking in the view and some are in the water swimming. A few are snorkeling to a nearby island.

A gentle breeze comes and goes. The breeze carries the wonderful scent of the salty ocean and I can smell the sand just beneath me. It smells just like the sea. I touch the sand and notice its dampness. It feels so fine and grainy in between my fingers and thumb.

What a wonderful way to spend a Holiday!

I pull out my writing material and begin to write as I feel a great story coming along.

By now, the two men have returned to the Hobiecats, this time with a young boy about age ten. They are all wearing life jackets. The instructor is now raising the colorful sail, which is bright yellow, red and blue in a partial sun ray design. He is gathering and securing all the other ropes to prepare them for their journey. He then checks their life jackets and is giving them basic instructions on how to operate the vessel.

There is a directional lever in the back of the boat. A rudder that helps guide the boat in the water. The instructor squats down in the sand. He draws with his finger in the sand. He is making a map for them to follow as he occasionally looks off and points into the distance. One man nods. They appear to have a plan now.

The two men and the instructor pull the boat backwards in the sand and into the water. The instructor stands aside as the two men and boy jump into the boat. The breeze gently carries the Hobiecat away from the sandy shore. One of the two men uses the rudder to guide themselves into the ocean waters. In a matter of moments the sailboat is sailing quickly and farther away. It moves seemingly effortless in the vast ocean waters. I watch the three of them intensely as they appear to get smaller and smaller. Another larger sail boat comes into view and I lose sight of them for a while.

The other boat moves on and they return to my view. They have left the nearby island waters and are heading towards a larger island which is quite far away. They have left the light blue waters and have joined the darker blue waters. The tall upright sail moves on so full of intent which seems overwhelming on a seemingly small boat. In my view they are like a tiny flea in the sand.

Before long I can no longer see the adventurers.

I continue relaxing and basking in the sun, awaiting in hopes that I am still here when the sailors return. I too have moved on into the darker blue waters.

I suddenly feel an intense shift of energy observing the American Hobiecat instructor looking my way with a serious sense of purpose. He must have felt my presence prior to, being quite a distance away. He is now heading my direction. Oh my! His destination does appear to be me!

My excitement stirs as I wonder what he wants.

He approaches his destination and bends down in the sand. His facial expression shows much curiosity and wonderment as we make eye contact.

"You are very intense," he says.

I respond with "I know."

He notices my notebook and pencil beside me. We discuss my experiential writings about my adventure today and his being in my story. He shares not being from these islands, but enjoys living and working here.

What beautiful scenery to be surrounded with every day. We chat about that a while without paying attention to time.

I look down at my watch and notice it's time for me to get back to the ferry for the last ride to St. Thomas.

I gather my things. We share a farewell as I rush off to the stop for the van to pick me up.

Until we meet again.

Printed in the United States
By Bookmasters